IN
GOOD TASTE

IN
GOOD TASTE

a creative collection of delicious,
easy to prepare, low-fat recipes
free of sugar and salt

by Tina Jencks

illustrations by Paula Morrison

introduction by Eileen Poole

Lancaster-Miller Publishers
Berkeley, California 1980

Copyright ©1980 by Lancaster-Miller, Inc.
3165 Adeline Street
Berkeley, California 94703

Printed and bound in the United States of America.

Library of Congress Catalog Number 80-82395
ISBN 0-89581-0204

Library of Congress Cataloging in Publication Data

Jencks, Tina.
        In good taste.

        1.   Low-fat diet--Recipes.   2.   Sugar-free diet--Recipes.
3.   Salt-free diet--Recipes.
I.   Title.
RM222.2.J46   641.5'63   80-82395
ISBN 0-89581-020-4

DEDICATION

This book is dedicated to Alan Jencks and Martin Inn, without whose patient support the book might not have been written.

ACKNOWLEDGEMENTS

We thankfully acknowledge the following people for their creative energies, so diligently applied: Janet King for editing, Sherry Alexander for book design and artistic advice, Michael Tolson for artistic advice, Tony Morse for assistance with the illustrations and Barbara Corso for typing.

We are grateful for recipe hints supplied by Alan Jencks, Martin Inn, Marion Rosen, Rita Robillard and Bruce Peterson.

Table of Contents

Vegetables

Fish

Poultry

Desserts

Six years ago an incident occurred which changed my life. I was badly frightened by the fact that my health had begun to falter at the age of twenty-five. I had developed infections, was in pain, and was told by a number of physicians that nothing could be done for me. No one seemed to know the reasons for my discomfort, and I was told to wait and see. I knew immediately that to wait and see was not the prescription for me.

After two months of searching for suitable alternative health care, I had lunch with a friend of mine and noticed that he looked terrific! His complexion seemed rosy and glowing and he was bursting with energy. Why this remarkable change, I wondered, so I asked what had brought about his new found vigor and health.

He was eager to explain this transformation and told me about his encounter with Eileen Poole, a highly acclaimed nutritionist and admirer of the late Dr. Henry G. Bieler. Bieler had devoted his medical career to helping his patients treat their ailments through changes in diet alone. "She's changed my life!" my friend said. "The greatest thing that's happened is that I no longer feel so helpless about growing old. I just might be able to enjoy the rest of my life without my body malfunctioning drastically!"

He told me about the diet she had prescribed for him which basically consisted of fresh fruits and vegetables, grains and whole grain products, and chicken and fish. Most importantly, added salt and sugar (including honey), alcohol and fried foods were totally eliminated from his diet. Instead of feeling deprived, he liked the challenge of this different approach to cooking and eating, and he felt inspired by his newfound fitness.

My own symptoms of ill health continued, and so I made an appointment to see Eileen Poole. I was immediately impressed with both her knowledge of the human body and her desire to lend support and direction to those wanting to regain or improve their health. Eileen predicted that my ailments could be cured by a change in eating habits. She prescribed a diet for me similar to the one she'd prescribed for my friend. The most essential aspect of this new diet was the elimination of added salt, sugar and significant amounts of fat from every dish I ate.

My health improved as my tastes gradually changed. I began to taste the natural flavor of many foods for the first time in my life. Amazing as it seemed to me then, my symptoms disappeared, and I now realize that there is nothing amazing about treating your body well and finding that it, in turn, will treat you well.

Though I was impressed, my dinner guests, however, were not. People are so used to salt, sugar and fat that a meal without these additives can seem uninviting. I was convinced that people could be just as pleased with my cooking style as with any other food preparation they were accustomed to. And so my inventions with food began.

I imagined exact flavors and then tried to combine foods to create these tastes. Coincidentally, I worked as a private cook during this time and frequently experimented on my employer. I was thrilled when he complimented me on a dish, never missing the salt, sugar and fats which I had omitted. As I kept track of the ingredients in these special meals, a collection of recipes gradually evolved.

This collection of recipes is not designed to prescribe a diet. It is, rather, a guide to the preparation of tasty, fresh foods. Hopefully, these recipes will serve not only as a guide to people on restrictive diets, but as an inspiration for those considering a change of menu for the purpose of improving their health.

Although all of my recipes are salt and sugar free, I have included some recipes using small amounts of fat. Where this occurs, clear indication is made and where possible, I have listed alternative ingredients. A couple of particularly rich dessert recipes have been included. These use whole milk or cream, and dried fruit as a sweetener. Because tastes and diets vary to such an extent, I wanted to cover a lot of ground, to demonstrate the possibilities open to everyone in adjusting to a healthy, new way of cooking.

Tina Jencks
Berkeley, California

Many of the foods included in these delicious recipes contain natural sugars, sodium and fats, all of which are essential in a healthy diet. These recipes contain limited amounts of fats and use no *added* salt or sugar.

Editor

INTRODUCTION

Many years ago, when not only the quality of my life had run out, but, it seemed, my very life itself, I had the good fortune to be led to Henry G. Bieler, M.D., author of *Food Is Your Best Medicine*. With his guidance, I learned a new approach to life through simplicity in diet.

I have been working with people now for many, many years; and the changes I have witnessed have been phenomenal. People come to see me for many reasons, but generally speaking, they want to feel better. Always I recommend, as did Dr. Bieler and many others in the field of nutrition, the elimination of salt, sugar (including its substitutes such as honey) and excess fats. As we know, there are also individual needs and intolerances as well, yet it is amazing to see the changes—the beginnings of a rejuvenation process—which even a slight alteration in diet can bring about. It is wonderful to see lines disappear from the face, to see the eyes become brighter, the figure more youthful, the hair shinier. People feel better, stronger, less tired. Not only does one experience these obvious physical benefits, but emotional benefits occur as well. I have noticed that people feel emotionally more sound as they become physically sound.

A change in diet is worthwhile not only because it may allow us longer lives, but because it adds depth to our lives as well. I always say that the goal in eating properly is not really to live forever, but to *really live* until we die.

People often tell me that a certain friend, despite eating a rich, salty diet, appears to be fit and healthy. Why? My response is that this friend is not you and that you have no way of knowing if he or she is really feeling so terrific. You are living for yourself, and the point is to be attentive to the messages—symptoms—given you by your own body. Years ago, when I was very ill, people around me considered me to be a person of immense energy. It was, therefore, quite interesting for me to observe how very little energy I actually had once I removed all of the props. Sugar, salt and other stimulants—including caffeine—do certainly give the body a charge; but we must not delude ourselves into thinking that this is energy.

The ideal situation for all of us is to know what our own bodies need and can handle. *This is health.* However, most of us love to eat and are addicted to certain foods or have been in the habit of using a good amount of salt and sugar in some form in our foods. These habits go back for many years—we become "hooked" at an early age—and frequently, from the time we are born, food is used for the wrong reasons.

Certainly hunger has little to do with most of our eating patterns. Often we are trying to fill an emotional void—and it can be a bottomless pit. I can remember so many times sitting down to eat and not wanting to ever stop. The satisfaction was in the act of eating, rather than in the food itself. Oddly enough, although this is a lifetime habit, we only seem to become aware of such habits when we make changes in our diets.

I am not happy with the word "diet." It sounds rather rigid, and also it has a temporary ring to it. After all, eating properly for your particular body needs is simply common sense. Besides, I get so many frantic calls from people in despair because they have "gone off" their diets. Not only do they feel uncomfortable physically, but they become quite wretched mentally as well. The guilt reaction can become even more negative than the incorrect food!

Having formed cooking and eating habits over a long period of time, people are initially at a loss as to how to make food tasty without salt, sugar and fat. Thus, I am constantly asked, "Is there a cookbook around which can help me start my change in diet?" Of course, as I have seen, eventually one's taste buds return, and even the most simple lettuce leaf tastes exquisite. This does take time, however, and so I'm happy to say that at last there is a cookbook that makes simple, unsugared, unsalted foods enticing and easy to prepare.

Tina has been gathering the material for this book through a period of many changes in her life, changes which came about as she began to pay attention to her own body messages a few years ago. It gives me great pleasure to be a part of this book, which started through that simple change of diet.

Eileen Poole

COOKING
NOTES

COOKING NOTES

Cooking with a Wok

Stir-frying in a wok thoroughly coats the meat or vegetables with oil, cooking them quickly while preserving their fresh taste. Since I like the taste which stir-frying lends to some dishes, I use a stir-fry-steam method, eliminating the need for the usual abundance of oil.

To use this method, coat the inner surface of the wok with 1 to 2 teaspoons of cooking oil. Use an absorbent cloth or paper towel to wipe away the excess. Place the wok, on its stand, over very high heat. As soon as the bowl of the wok begins to smoke *slightly,* add meat and vegetables. Stir and toss quickly for 2 to 3 minutes. Add 1/4 to 1/2 cup liquid and cover. The cooking process will be completed by the steam which gathers under the lid. Steaming time is usually 3 to 8 minutes, depending on the ingredients. Stir at least once while steaming to prevent food from sticking to the bottom of the wok.

Another way to achieve the same effect is to first steam your vegetables until just done and then add them to the oiled wok. Add seasoning, if any, stir and toss quickly for 2 to 3 minutes, then serve.

Of course, a frying pan may be substituted to achieve a similar effect.

Cooking with Steam

It is generally accepted that the best way to cook vegetables is to steam them. When steamed, they don't lose their nutritive value to the water (as in boiling), and they retain their color. Also, they seem to suffer less from over-cooking when prepared this way.

The most convenient of the many items available in steaming equipment is the stainless steel basket steamer, a collapsible multipetaled metal basket which sits up on three small legs. This basket fits into any saucepan over 6" in diameter and contains the vegetables, supported above 2" of boiling water.

Alternately, a tiered bamboo steamer can be placed over a wok. This method takes a bit longer because the steam has farther to travel, but it offers a great convenience: foods in the top tier will cook more slowly than those in the bottom one, allowing the preparation of foods requiring different cooking times in only one pan.

Standard kitchen utensils can also be used. For example, a double boiler or simply a large strainer hooked over the rim of a saucepan serves well as a steamer. Whatever equipment is used, the saucepan should be covered and vegetable cooking time will vary from 3 to 12 minutes.

A hint for steaming: I often place romaine lettuce or cabbage leaves in the steamer basket underneath the food I am preparing as a catch-all, as some steamers have rather large openings for the steam. This also prevents a "woody" taste from getting into the food if a bamboo steamer is used.

COOKING NOTES

Items to Keep on Hand

In creating meals, I emphasize the fresh flavor of the foods themselves. I have come to rely on certain special kitchen tools and provisions for the preparation of my recipes.

Special Cooking Equipment:
- A wok or large frying pan (See *Cooking with a Wok*)
- A blender or food processor
- A steamer—either a stainless steel basket steamer or a tiered bamboo steamer which fits over a wok (See *Cooking with Steam*)

Assorted Staples:
- Apple Juice
- Chicken broth (see *Basic Chicken Broth* recipe). Use as a substitute for oil in dressings.
- Toasted sesame oil. This should be purchased *pre-toasted*. It is dark brown in color and has a fabulous taste!
- Kanten (see *About Kanten*)
- Low-sodium baking powder
- Unsalted (sweet) butter (optional)

I like to stock a variety of grains. Some suggestions are:
- rice and sweet rice
- millet
- buckwheat
- barley
- rye flakes

COOKING NOTES

I also recommend keeping a variety of flours on hand.
Those with the greatest versatility are:
- whole wheat
- rice
- rye
- millet

An assortment of herbs and spices should be readily
available to jazz up a dish according to individual taste.
Those I use most are:
- cayenne pepper
- cumin
- curry
- dill
- oregano
- rosemary
- sage
- sweet basil
- tarragon
- allspice
- cardamon
- cinnamon
- cloves
- nutmeg
- fresh ginger

COOKING NOTES

About Kanten

Kanten (or "agar-agar") is a gelling agent often used in Oriental cooking. Derived from sea weed which has been boiled down and pressed into bars, Kanten is tasteless, and is a good substitute for gelatin, an animal product.

I prefer Kanten to gelatin, as it makes smoother sauces and is less likely to create lumps. Regular gelatin, however, may be substituted where Kanten is called for.

Note

Always read the recipe *carefully* before you begin to cook. That way you can determine preparation time and plan a necessary trip to the market.

I have indicated the approximate number of people each recipe will serve, but of course, this quantity will vary with appetite and eating style.

T. J.

SOUPS

SOUPS

Basic Chicken Broth

A key item to have on hand! Chicken broth can be used as a quick soup as well as a component of salad dressing or sauce. It is useful warm or cold, and the meat can of course be saved for use in many other dishes.

> 1 whole chicken, cut up
> 1 small onion, cut into chunks
> 2 celery stalks, cut into chunks
> 1 carrot, cut into chunks

Put all ingredients into a large, deep saucepan or stockpot and cover with water. Heat to a boil, then reduce heat to low and cook, covered, for 1 1/2 hours, or until meat loosens somewhat from the bones. Remove chicken and vegetables from pan. Discard vegetables, chicken skin and bones, saving meat for another dish. Refrigerate broth for at least 12 hours or until the chicken fat has hardened over the surface of the broth. Skim off fat chunks with a spoon. The broth is now ready.

Note: Some broths turn out more gelatinous than others, and may need to be reheated slightly to liquify.

Ginger Chicken Soup

Delicate and delicious!

       4 cups chicken broth
       1 cucumber
       2 green onions
       1 tsp. fresh ginger, grated
       1/2 tsp. sweet basil

Heat broth in a saucepan over medium heat. Peel and slice cucumber and add to broth. Add ginger and basil and simmer until cucumber is very tender when pierced with a fork.

Run the soup through a blender and return to saucepan. Add finely chopped green onions. Simmer 5 more minutes.

Serves 4.

SOUPS

Tomato-Dill Soup

Delicious—even better after storing a day or two.

> 4 large potatoes, peeled and cut into chunks
> 4 large tomatoes, sliced
> 1 - 12 oz. can unsalted tomato juice
> 1 yellow or white onion, peeled and sliced
> 4 stalks celery, chopped
> 1 tsp. dill
> 1 pinch cayenne pepper
> 1/2 cup water

Place all ingredients in a large saucepan and simmer, covered, over medium heat for 1/2 hour.

Pour contents of saucepan into a blender and puree. Serve immediately, or return to saucepan to keep warm.

Serves 4.

SOUPS

Gazpacho

This is a unique version of the renowned cold Spanish soup.

> 1/2 bunch romaine lettuce
> 1 green pepper, seeded and sliced
> 2 medium tomatoes, chopped
> 1/2 cucumber, peeled
> 1/2 small avocado, peeled and pitted
> 2 limes

Puree lettuce, pepper, tomatoes, cucumber and avocado in a blender. Pour into serving bowls. Squeeze 1/2 lime over each serving and stir.

Serves 4.

SOUPS

Asparagus-Vegetable Soup

This soup needs no herbs or spices—tastes great as is!

        1 bunch asparagus
        6 stalks celery, chopped into chunks
        1 bunch fresh spinach
        2 cups water

Clean asparagus and remove the thick bottom part of the stalk. Place in saucepan with water and begin simmering over medium heat. Add celery and cook until just tender, about 8 minutes.

Clean spinach thoroughly and chop off bottom of stems. Add to other vegetables and cook 2 to 3 minutes longer, until spinach is limp but still bright green.

Puree vegetables with cooking water in a blender. Reheat.

Serves 3.

Lemon Vegetable Soup

Surprisingly filling! Serve with a light meal.

3 medium-sized tomatoes, sliced
4 scallop squash, sliced (the round, green ones with the scalloped edges)
4 small leeks, chopped, with root end removed (rinse carefully—dirt tends to hide between layers)
1 large cucumber, peeled and chopped
2 tsp. oregano
Juice of one whole lemon
1 lemon, thinly sliced
2 cups water

Mix all ingredients, except lemon slices, in a saucepan. Bring to a boil, then simmer over medium-low heat for 10 minutes. Remove a few leek slices for use as a garnish. Blend remaining vegetables and water. Steam lemon slices for 1 minute and use with leek slices as garnish.

Serves 4 to 6.

SOUPS

Minestrone Soup

Makes a filling meal served with salad.

2-3 cups broth (see *Basic Chicken Broth*)
1 yellow onion, sliced
1/4 cup parsley, minced
1 tsp. oregano
2 pinches cayenne
4 tomatoes, chopped into chunks
4 stalks celery, chopped
2 zucchini, grated
1 cup okra, chopped
Fresh corn cut from 2 large cobs
2 cups large whole wheat shell noodles,
   cooked

Pour 1/4 cup of the chicken broth into a large saucepan. Add onion, parsley, oregano and cayenne and simmer and stir over medium heat until the onion seems limp, about 3 to 5 minutes.

Puree 1/2 of the chopped tomatoes and 1/2 of the chopped celery in a blender with 1 cup of the chicken broth. Add to saucepan.

Add remaining vegetables and broth. Continue to simmer over medium heat until liquid boils, then turn heat down to low. Cover and continue to simmer for 20 minutes.

Add cooked noodles and if desired, garnish with fresh parsley.

Serves 4.

SOUPS

Potato-Leek Soup

A delicious non-dairy "cream" soup.

    4 large potatoes, peeled and sliced
    3 leeks, thoroughly cleaned and
        chopped into large pieces
    6 stalks celery, chopped
    1 clove garlic, minced
    1 tsp. thyme
    1 bay leaf

Put potatoes, leeks, celery, garlic, thyme and bay leaf into a saucepan. Add just enough water to cover vegetables—about 3 cups should do. Simmer over medium heat until all vegetables are soft, about 15 to 20 minutes. Remove pan from heat and discard bay leaf.

Puree contents of saucepan in a blender, return to pan, heat and serve.

Serves 4 to 6.

Summer Squash Stew

This hearty soup combines three favorite summer squashes.

>   1 clove garlic, minced
>   3 cups broth (see *Basic Chicken Broth*)
>   3 zucchini, thinly sliced
>   3 crookneck squash, thinly sliced
>   6 scallop squash, thinly sliced
>   3 green onions, chopped

Heat 1 cup of the chicken broth with garlic in a saucepan. Simmer for 10 minutes. Add remaining broth and squash and simmer for another 5 to 7 minutes until squash is just tender.

Serves 4.

SALADS

SALADS

Wilted Spinach

This dish can serve either as salad or as the meal's vegetable.

> 1 bunch spinach
> 3-4 zucchini
> 2 green onions
> Chicken Broth Dressing (see *Salad Dressings*)

Wash spinach thoroughly and remove large stems. Remove stem ends from zucchini, then slice into very thin rounds, preferably using the slicing notch on a grater. Finely chop the green onions. Toss all greens together. Heat Chicken Broth Dressing. Pour over greens and serve immediately.

Serves 4.

Watercress Salad with Pine Nuts

Goes well with any main course.

>   1 head romaine lettuce
>   1 bunch watercress
>   5 large carrots, grated
>   1/2 cup pine nuts
>   Sesame Dressing (see *Salad Dressings*)

Slice the head of lettuce horizontally into thin shreds. Remove thicker stems from watercress and discard. Finely chop the rest of the watercress and toss with carrots and lettuce in a large bowl. Mix in the pine nuts and add dressing.

Serves 6.

SALADS

Eileen's Egg Salad

*A delicious and unusual breakfast or lunch on a hot
day. This dish makes its own sauce.*

Per person, use:
1/3 head romaine lettuce
1 small or 1/2 large raw zucchini, grated
5 parsley sprigs, finely chopped
1/2 green pepper, thinly sliced
1 stalk celery, finely chopped
2-3 Tbs. Lemon and Apple Juice
    Dressing (see *Salad Dressings*)
2 eggs, soft-boiled and peeled

Make a salad with the greens and cover with dressing. Set the two peeled, soft-boiled eggs on top of the
salad and slice into them, allowing the yolk to run over
the salad.

Tabouli

Rice gives this traditional Near Eastern grain salad a sweeter taste than the usual bulgar wheat.

2 cups short grain brown rice, uncooked
2 bunches spinach
2 sweet red onions, finely sliced
2 green peppers, finely sliced
1/2 lb. mushrooms, finely sliced
1 Tbs. tarragon
1 Tbs. sweet basil
1 tsp. garlic powder
1 head romaine lettuce

Dressing:
1/4 cup olive oil
Juice of 5 lemons

Cook the rice and set aside to cool. Place spinach in boiling water for one minute and drain well.

Steam onions, peppers and mushrooms together until lightly cooked. Mix rice, vegetables and herbs together in a large bowl and set in refrigerator to chill for about an hour.

Mix together oil and lemon dressing and stir in just before serving. Serve the salad arranged on a bed of romaine lettuce leaves.

Serves 6 to 8.

SALADS

Salade Niçoise

Great picnic fare, this dish can be easily assembled on the spot.

 4 red potatoes, boiled until just done,
    peeled and cubed
 1/2 lb. green beans, cooked
 1- 6 1/2 oz. can of low-sodium tuna,
    drained, or fresh cooked tuna
 2 heads of lettuce (romaine is best)
 Cherry tomatoes
 Sprigs of parsley

 Dressing:
 1/2 cup apple juice
 1/2 cup cider vinegar
 1 bunch green onions, sliced crosswise
    very thinly
 1 1/2 Tbs. dill weed

Mix dressing ingredients thoroughly and set aside.

Marinate potatoes in about 1/3 of the dressing, and the beans and tuna together in another third.

Wash, dry thoroughly and tear up lettuce. Toss in a large bowl with the remainder of the dressing.

Arrange the potato salad on the lettuce and place beans and tuna on top. Garnish with tomatoes and parsley.

Serves 8.

Salade Niçoise

SALADS

Red and Green Salad

This colorful salad is lovely as a party buffet dish.

> 1/2 lb. string beans
> 2 large red bell peppers
> 1/2 cup slivered almonds (optional)
> Lemon-Apple Juice Dressing (see *Salad Dressings*)

Clean string beans and cut each into two or three pieces. Cut stems off peppers, remove pith and seeds, and slice into long strips about 1/4" wide. Steam beans and peppers together for about 5 minutes, until just barely cooked. (The colors of the vegetables should still be bright—if they seem faded, they have been cooked too long.)

Transfer to a serving bowl and chill. Dress with Lemon-Apple Juice Dressing. Sprinkle almonds over the top, and serve.

Serves 4.

Gourmet Potato Salad

For best results, make this salad the night before you plan to serve it.

> 10-12 potatoes (White Rose boiling
>   potatoes are best)
> 1 small yellow onion
> 1 cup chicken broth, hot (see *Basic
>   Chicken Broth*)
> Juice from 2 lemons
> 1/2 tsp. dill

Boil the potatoes for a 1/2 hour, until easily pierced with a fork. Remove from water and cool for about 20 minutes, then peel and slice about 1/4" thick and place in a large serving bowl.

Peel the onion, then grate it into the potatoes, using largest holes on grater. Add chicken broth, lemon juice and dill. Mix well.

Refrigerate overnight. Turn the salad in the bowl several times before serving.

Serves 6 to 8.

SALADS

Apple, Beet and Potato Salad

A colorful "Waldorf alternative."

> 4 small whole fresh beets
> 2 large White Rose or other boiling
>   potatoes
> 2 Pippin apples, cored
> Juice from 2 small lemons
> 1/2 tsp. olive oil

Boil beets and potatoes for 1/2 hour or until easily pierced with a fork. Steam apples for 15 to 20 minutes.

Peel beets, potatoes and apples, then cube. Mix together in a serving bowl. Mix lemon juice and olive oil and add. Mix again. Chill before serving.

Serves 4.

Marinated Broccoli Salad

If you wish to leave the oil out of the marinade, use 2 teaspoons apple juice instead.

    1 bunch broccoli (about 1 1/2 lbs.)
    1 shallot, minced
    6-8 large mushrooms, thinly sliced
    1/2 tsp. bouquet garni
    3-4 Tbs. apple cider vinegar
    1 1/2 tsp. safflower or peanut oil

Break broccoli into small flowers and chop upper stems into small pieces. Steam with shallots for 5 minutes, until just soft but not paled in color. Add mushrooms and steam for an additional 3 minutes.

Mix steamed vegetables in a serving bowl. Add bouquet garni, vinegar and oil. Mix well. Chill, turning occasionally, for at least 1 hour before serving.

Serves 6.

SALADS

Tomato Aspic

A unique molded salad.

>3 cups unsalted tomato juice
>1 stick kanten (see *Cooking Notes*)
>Juice of 1 lemon
>Juice from 2 cloves of garlic, pressed
>1 pinch cayenne pepper
>3 stalks celery, finely diced
>2 green onions, finely diced
>1 lb. bay (small) shrimp

Pour tomato juice into saucepan. Break kanten into 2 or 3 chunks and add to juice. Add lemon, garlic juice and cayenne, and cook over medium-low heat until kanten is completely dissolved, at least 20 minutes.

Remove from heat and add diced vegetables and shrimp. Place in refrigerator for 10 minutes, or until aspic has thickened slightly but is still liquid.

Remove from refrigerator and stir, distributing vegetables and shrimp throughout the aspic. Pour into aspic mold and refrigerate for at least 1 hour, or until firm.

To unmold, immerse three quarters of the way in hot (but not boiling) water. As soon as aspic loosens slightly, turn onto serving plate.

Serves 6.

Salad Dressings

Chicken broth works beautifully as a substitute for oil in salad dressings. Tastes great!

Chicken Broth Dressing

1 cup chicken broth (see *Basic Chicken Broth*)
Juice of 1 lemon or 1 Tbs. vinegar
1/4 tsp. dried sweet basil

Mix thoroughly.

Sesame Dressing

1/2 cup apple juice
1 Tbs. apple cider vinegar
4 drops toasted sesame oil
1/4 tsp. dried marjoram

Mix thoroughly.

SALADS

Avocado Dressing

1 whole ripe avocado, pitted,
 peeled and mashed
1 Tbs. apple cider vinegar
1/2 cup chicken broth (see
 Basic Chicken Broth)
1 pinch ground cumin seed
1 pinch cayenne pepper

Combine ingredients in a blender.

Lemon-Apple Juice Dressing

A light, sweet dressing.

1/2 cup apple juice
Juice from 1 lemon

Mix thoroughly.

Tomato Dressing

1/2 cup apple juice
1 Tbs. apple cider vinegar
1 soft, ripe tomato, pureed
1/4 tsp. thyme
1 tsp. olive oil

Combine ingredients in a blender.

VEGETABLES

VEGETABLES

Fresh Mint Peas

This dish goes especially well with chicken or turkey.

> 2 lbs. fresh peas, shelled or 2-10 oz.
>   packages frozen peas
> 3 fresh spearmint leaves
>   (not peppermint)

Chop the spearmint leaves into very small pieces and mix with uncooked peas. Steam peas with mint for 3 to 5 minutes.

Serves 4 to 6.

Cauliflower with Lemon Sauce

Impressive, yet easy.

       1 large cauliflower
       2 Tbs. unsalted (sweet) butter
       1 - 1 1/2 Tbs. flour
       Juice from one lemon

Place whole cauliflower in a saucepan which fits just around it but leaves several inches free at the top. Cover with water and simmer over medium–low heat for 20 to 25 minutes or until easily pierced with a fork, but not mushy. Remove cauliflower from pan and place on a serving platter. Save cooking water.

Melt butter in a saucepan. Slowly add the flour, beating quickly with a wire whip to form a smooth, creamy roux. Slowly add cauliflower cooking water, 1/4 cup at a time, stirring constantly, until a creamy, thin sauce has formed. (Use approximately 1 1/2 - 2 cups of the cauliflower water.) Add lemon juice and cook for another 3 minutes.

Pour sauce over cauliflower and serve.

Serves 4 to 6.

VEGETABLES

Savoy Cabbage with Apples

I find savoy cabbage to have much more flavor than regular cabbage. A darker green than regular cabbage, the leaves of the savoy variety are also more textured.

> 1 small head savoy cabbage, chopped
> into thin shreds
> 3 Pippin apples, peeled and grated (use
> largest grater holes)
> 1 red onion, thinly sliced
> 1 tsp. cinnamon

Mix cabbage, onion and apple together. Sprinkle with cinnamon and mix again. Steam for 5 to 6 minutes or until cabbage is tender.

Serves 6.

Swiss Chard with Lemon and Garlic

1 bunch chard, red or white stalk,
    washed thoroughly
2 tsp. unflavored cooking oil (peanut oil
    works best)
2 cloves garlic, minced
Juice from 1 large lemon

Remove an inch or two of stem from chard, then slice into 2" wide strips, horizontally. Steam for 5 minutes.

Heat oil in a wok or large frying pan (see *Cooking Notes*). Add minced garlic and cook for 2 minutes. Add steamed chard and lemon juice and stir and toss for another 2 minutes.

Serves 4.

VEGETABLES

Winter Squash Special

Rich tasting and very nutritious!

    1 whole acorn (Danish) squash
    1 cup apple or pear juice
    1 apple, stewed, peeled, cored and
        pureed (or 1/2 cup unsweetened
        applesauce)
    Unsalted (sweet) butter

Bake squash whole on a rack in a 375° oven for 1 to 1 1/2 hours. (Squash is done when easily pierced with a fork.) Remove the meat from the squash, discarding skin and seeds. Place squash meat in a shallow baking dish and mash vigorously along with juice and apple.

Dot with sweet butter and broil until the squash is browned.

Serves 3.

Winter Squash Party Variation

1 whole butternut squash
2/3 cup unsweetened pineapple juice
1 cup crushed pineapple, canned or
    chopped fresh
1 cup unsweetened *large* flake
    coconut, loosely packed

Prepare squash as in previous recipe. Instead of broiling with butter, top with coconut and bake in 375° oven until coconut turns golden brown.

Serves 4.

VEGETABLES

Bok Choy and Yellow Squash

Toasted sesame oil has a wonderful flavor and it's very strong. Use only in small amounts.

> 1 bunch bok choy
> 3 large yellow (crookneck) squash,
>   sliced into 1/4" rounds
> 2 tsp. toasted sesame oil
> 1/4 -1/2 cup water

Clean bok choy and remove bottom 3 to 4" of stalk. Slice into 2" chunks, leaves and all.

Heat a wok or large frying pan (see *Cooking Notes*) over high heat and add oil, spreading thinly with paper towel or absorbent cloth. (The aim is to use as little oil as possible, yet add special flavor to the vegetables, and to keep them from sticking to the pan.) As soon as the pan begins to smoke slightly, add vegetables. Stir and toss quickly for about 2 minutes. Add 1/4 cup water and cover. Cook for 3 to 4 minutes longer, adding liquid as necessary to keep vegetables from sticking to pan.

Remove to a serving dish and pour extra pan juices over vegetables.

Serves 4.

Stuffed Tomatoes

A spicy dish without spice!

>   6-8 medium-sized tomatoes, as round
>   as possible
>   5 Japanese eggplants, or 1/2 large
>   eggplant chopped into small chunks
>   2 cloves garlic, finely chopped or
>   pressed
>   1/2 cup grated daikon radish (or
>   another hot radish)
>   2 eggs
>   1/4 cup whole wheat flour

Slice tops off tomatoes, making the cut about 1/4" down the side of the tomato, thus removing a cap-shaped piece. Scoop out insides with a spoon. Set tomato "shells" aside.

Place eggplant in blender with chopped garlic, grated radish and eggs. Blend. Add flour and blend on slowest speed.

Stuff tomatoes with blended mixture, place in a large baking dish and bake at 350° for 20 minutes.

Serves 6.

VEGETABLES

Snow Peas and Cucumber with Black Mushrooms

Snow Peas and Cucumber with Black Mushrooms

A different combination for a special meal.

- 8 - 12 dried black mushrooms (about 2 per person)
- 1/4 – 1/2 cup water from soaking mushrooms (see instructions below)
- 2 tsp. toasted sesame oil
- 1/2 lb. snow peas, cleaned, with stems and strings removed
- 2 cucumbers, peeled and sliced into long thin spears

Remove stems from dried black mushrooms. Place mushrooms in a bowl and pour enough boiling water over them to just cover. Soak for 5 minutes.

Heat a wok or large frying pan over high heat and add oil, spreading thinly over the insides of the wok or pan with paper towel or absorbent cloth. As soon as the pan begins to smoke slightly, add vegetables. Stir and toss quickly for about 2 minutes.

Add 1/4 cup mushroom–soaking water and cover. Cook for 3 to 4 minutes longer with just enough liquid to keep vegetables from sticking to pan. Remove to a serving dish and pour extra pan juices over vegetables.

Serves 4 to 6.

VEGETABLES

Excellent Eggplant

A tasty dish, either hot or cold.

      1 eggplant
      2 tsp. toasted sesame oil
      1 clove garlic, minced
      2 tsp. grated fresh ginger
      1/4 cup rice wine vinegar
      1/2 tsp. cayenne pepper
      1 head romaine lettuce (if dish is served
         cold)

Cut eggplant in half width-wise, then slice into long spears about 3/4" thick. Steam until thoroughly cooked, about 5 to 8 minutes, and remove from heat.

Heat toasted sesame oil in a wok or large frying pan, spreading it around to coat the inner bowl evenly (see *Cooking Notes*).

Add garlic and stir for 2 minutes, then add steamed eggplant and ginger and continue to stir for another 3 to 5 minutes.

Remove wok or pan from heat. Add vinegar and toss thoroughly. Sprinkle with cayenne pepper. Serve hot, or chill in refrigerator overnight, then serve the following day, rolling up the eggplant in romaine lettuce leaves.

Serves 4.

VEGETABLES

Vegetable Curry

This combination of vegetables can be varied to produce an array of subtle flavors, colors and textures.

1 medium-sized head of cauliflower,
  cut into bite-sized chunks
2 carrots, sliced into 1/4" rounds
1/2 lb. mushrooms, cut into chunks
2 zucchini, cut into chunks
2 yellow (crookneck) squash

Curry Sauce:
1 Tbs. curry powder (for rather mild
  curry)
1 onion, coarsely chopped
2 apples, peeled, cored and chopped
6 big celery stalks, deveined and sliced
1 1/2 cups water
1 1/2 cups apple juice

To prepare the curry sauce, first warm the curry powder in a large, dry saucepan, shaking the pan above a high flame for about 30 seconds. Set aside to cool a bit. Combine onions, apples, celery, juice and water with curry in the pan. Bring to a boil, then simmer, covered for about 15 minutes. Puree in a blender.

Add cauliflower and carrots to the sauce. Return to a boil, then cover and simmer for about 10 minutes, or until cauliflower and carrots are almost tender. Add remaining vegetables and cook about 10 minutes.

Serve on rice with *Apple Chutney* (see next recipe).

To save time, you may steam the vegetables while preparing the curry sauce, but the vegetables should stand in the sauce for a while to marry the flavors.

Serves 6.

VEGETABLES

Apple Chutney

Chutney is the traditional accompaniment to Indian curried dishes. It is also good on morning toast.

3 apples, peeled, cored and coarsely
   chopped
1/2 cup apple juice
1 inch ginger root, peeled
1 inch of tamarind or 2 Tbs. cider
   vinegar and 1/3 cup raisins
   (Tamarind is a dark, sour fruit,
   marketed in a pressed block.)

Put apples in a saucepan with the juice. Add ginger root, squeezed through a garlic press. Add the tamarind cut in pieces or if it's unavailable, use vinegar and raisins.

Simmer, covered, until apples are tender. Mash about half the apples with a fork or potato masher.

Serve as is or chilled.

Stuffed Zucchini

One half of a zucchini per person is ample. This makes a good side dish for a simple chicken or fish recipe, or an interesting breakfast dish.

3 large zucchini, about 10" long
1 large tomato, diced
2 pieces of toast, preferably whole
    wheat or rye, diced
1 Tbs. minced parsley
1 clove garlic, minced
1 egg, beaten

Slice zucchini in half lengthwise. Steam for about 3 to 4 minutes or until just beginning to soften. Remove from steamer and scrape out the center, leaving a shell about 1/4" thick. Reserve zucchini meat.

Mix tomatoes, toast, parsley and garlic with zucchini meat, then add egg and mix again. Fill each zucchini half with this mixture. Bake for 15 minutes in a pre-heated 350° oven, then broil for a couple of minutes to brown the tops.

Serves 6.

FISH

FISH

Salmon Salad

A quick, beautiful and satisfying lunch for a warm day.

> 1 lb. fresh salmon filets
> 1 head romaine lettuce
> 4 scallions, chopped
> 1 cucumber, thinly sliced
> 4 stalks celery
> Alfalfa sprouts
> 2 green peppers
> 2 tsp. dill
> 1 tsp. thyme
> 1/2 lb. cooked bay shrimp
> Juice of 2 lemons
> 1 1/2 Tbs. olive oil

Steam salmon very lightly. The bright red color of the outer meat will turn pink but the inside meat should still appear reddish. Mix the salad greens with the herbs in a large bowl. Flake the steamed salmon into the salad and add shrimp. Chill. Mix lemon and oil and dress salad, tossing thoroughly.

Serves 4 to 6.

Poached Fish with Green Winter Sauce

Dinner at a Chinese restaurant inspired the name of the sauce for this dish.

2–4 filets of fresh, white fish (sole, halibut or red snapper)

Sauce:
2 leeks, chopped
2 cloves garlic, peeled and chopped
1 cup water
1 tsp. basil
1 pinch curry powder
1 Tbs. sweet butter
Chopped fresh chives or parsley for garnish
Bay shrimp for garnish (optional)

Poach fish by placing in a pan with just enough water to cover, then simmer, covered for 5 to 10 minutes.

Cook leeks and garlic in water along with spices. Remove from heat and add butter, allowing it to melt into the liquid. Combine in a blender with water from the poached fish. Serve sauce over fish with chopped fresh chives or parsley. A few bay shrimp make a decorative garnish.

Serves 2 to 4.

FISH

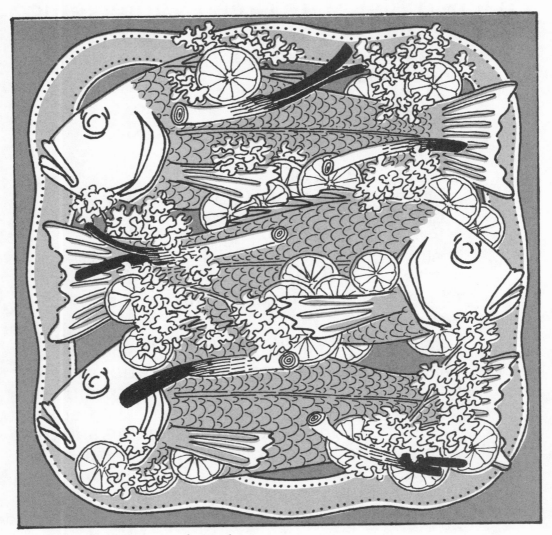

Chinese Steamed Fish

Chinese Steamed Fish

This wonderful dish makes its own sauce!

> 1 whole, cleaned rock cod or red
> snapper
> Lemon, thinly sliced
> Juice of 1/2 lemon
> Ginger root, cut into toothpick-like
> slivers, about 1 Tbs.
> Green onion, slit in half lengthwise and
> cut into 2" sections
> Cayenne pepper
> Parsley

Choose very fresh fish, small enough to fit with head and tail intact on a dinner plate (about 10" or smaller). Elevate the plate on a tin can (with both ends removed) inside your largest pot so that steam may circulate around the fish.

Insert lemon slices into the fish, and cover the top with lemon, ginger and green onions to taste. Sprinkle very lightly with cayenne pepper.

Steam until done, about 7 to 10 minutes. Garnish with parsley.

Serves 4.

FISH

Broiled Steelhead

Steelhead is not as rich as salmon and has a wonderful flavor. Particularly good on salmon or steelhead, the garlic-parsley-lemon combination works on other fish as well.

        4 steelhead steaks, about 1/2" thick
        2 cloves garlic, minced
        1 Tbs. parsley, minced
        Juice of 2 lemons

Place the steaks on a flat broiling pan. Cover with half of the garlic, parsley and lemon juice. Broil for 4 to 5 minutes. Turn steaks over, cover with remaining mixture and broil for another 4 to 5 minutes.

Serves 4.

Fish and Noodle Casserole

6 oz. whole wheat (or other) shell
    noodles, uncooked

1 1/2 - 2 lbs. cod or red snapper filets
2 cloves garlic, peeled and pressed
Juice from 2 lemons
1 large sprig parsley, minced
1 cup water

Cook noodles for 10 to 15 minutes or until soft. Drain.
Arrange filets in a "broil-proof" shallow baking dish.
Pour lemon juice over fish, then add pressed garlic and
parsley to the liquid surrounding the fish. Add water
and broil for about 3 to 4 minutes, then flip filets and
broil for another 3 to 4 minutes. Flake fish into chunks,
carefully removing any small bones.

Combine noodles, fish and cooking juices in a serving dish. Mix well and serve.

Serves 4.

FISH

Stuffed Red Snapper

Serve with a crisp green salad for a lovely party meal.

2 medium-sized zucchini, sliced into
  1/2" rounds
1 sweet green chili, with seeds
  removed, chopped
6-8 mushrooms, chopped into chunks
1 small red onion, peeled and diced
1/4 tsp. chili powder
1/2 tsp. oregano
1 whole, cleaned red snapper, 3-4 lbs.
2 cups cooked brown rice
1 cup water

Steam together zucchini, chili, mushrooms and onion until soft, about 6-8 minutes. Remove from heat.

Add chili powder and oregano to cooked rice and mix well. Then combine with zucchini, chili, mushrooms and onions. Stuff fish with this mixture.

Set fish into a small baking dish, adding the water to the bottom of the dish. Bake, uncovered, in a preheated 350° oven for 45 minutes, or until fish flakes easily.

Serves 4.

Barbecue-Grilled Halibut

Grilling over a barbecue or hibachi gives special flavor to this fish. Marinated halibut may also be broiled.

6 halibut steaks (thick cuts if possible)
Juice from 2 lemons
1 clove garlic, pressed or minced
3 drops toasted sesame oil

Mix the lemon juice, garlic and toasted sesame oil together in a small saucepan and cook over low heat for 3 to 4 minutes. Remove from heat, pour into a blender and puree.

Brush mixture over both sides of each halibut steak and set on grill over hot coals. Continue to brush mixture onto the steaks as they cook. Allow about 4 to 6 minutes per side, depending upon the thickness of the steaks. Remove to a large platter and serve.

Serves 6.

FISH

Yosenabe

Yosenabe in Japanese means "gathering of everything." Substitute ingredients as you like in this flavorful dish.

8 dried black mushrooms, with stems removed
1 cup hot water
1 bunch green onions
1 1/2 lbs. fish steaks or filets (tuna, sea bass, rock cod or snapper), cut into chunks
1 carrot, sliced into 1/8" rounds
1 small Napa (Chinese) cabbage, sliced crosswise into 1" strips
1 bunch spinach
1 handful bean sprouts
1 small can bamboo shoots
1/4 lb. rice sticks or bean threads (transparent noodles)

Soak mushrooms in hot water for about 10 minutes while preparing the other ingredients.

Cut green onions in half lengthwise and then into 2" sections. Arrange with remaining ingredients in a wok or large, shallow pan. Add mushroom-soaking liquid and water to just cover. Bring to a boil, then simmer for about 10 minutes.

Yosenabe is a meal in itself, and it can be served family style. Each diner is given chopsticks, a soup spoon (don't waste the broth!) and a bowl of rice or buckwheat noodles, and eats directly from the cooking pot, placed in the center of the table.

Serves 4.

FISH

Ceviche

In this South American dish, the acid from the lemon and lime juice "cooks" the fish as it marinates.

1 lb. filet of sole
1 red onion, very thinly sliced
1 clove garlic, minced
2 tsp. fresh sweet basil, finely minced
1 pinch chili powder
1/2 cup lemon juice
1/4 cup lime juice

Lay filets flat on a platter which has a slight rim. Distribute onion, garlic and basil evenly over them and sprinkle with chili powder. Mix lemon and lime juice and pour over filets.

Cover plate with plastic wrap and refrigerate for about 7 hours, turning once at mid point. Remove from juice and serve with the onions.

Serves 4.

Bouillabaisse

FISH

Bouillabaisse

A hearty, satisfying meal.

6 clams in shell
1/4 cup olive oil (optional—vegetables
  may be simmered in 1 cup of water
  instead)
3 leeks, thinly sliced
2 cloves garlic, minced
1/2 lb. fresh mushrooms, sliced
4 tomatoes
1 cup red wine or 1 cup carrot-celery
  juice mixed with the juice of 1 small
  lemon
2 green peppers, thinly sliced
3 medium zucchini, thinly sliced
1 tsp. basil
Pinch cayenne
1/2 lb. prawns
1/2 lb. scallops or crab meat
1/2 lb. sea bass
1/2 lb. red snapper or ling cod

Steam clams in 2 cups water until their shells open. Set aside and reserve liquid.

Heat olive oil for a minute in a large stewing pot, then add leeks, garlic and mushrooms. Cover and cook over low heat.

Puree tomatoes with the clam water and wine or vegetable juice in a blender, then add to vegetables. Add basil and cayenne. Cook for 20 minutes, stirring occasionally. Add zucchini and green peppers and continue cooking for 6 minutes.

Remove prawns from shells and chop fish into bite-sized pieces, removing skin from bass and any small bones from snapper or cod. Add all fish, clams included, and simmer for another 5 minutes.

Serves 6 to 8.

FISH

Paella

Another meal in itself—and very elegant!

1 1/2 cups raw brown rice
1 large yellow onion, sliced
3 large tomatoes, chopped
2 medium sized sweet jalapeño
  peppers, sliced, with seeds removed
1 tsp. olive oil (optional)
1-12 oz. can unsalted tomato juice
1 tsp. thyme
1/2 tsp. cumin
2 zucchini, grated
2 lbs. red snapper filets, cut into chunks
  (Be careful to remove any small
  bones.)
1/2 lb. cooked bay shrimp or 1/2 lb.
  prawns, shelled and chopped into
  small chunks
1 lb. fresh peas, shelled or 1-10 oz.
  package frozen peas

Begin cooking the rice. (It usually takes 45 minutes to 1 hour.)

Place onion, tomato and peppers in a large stockpot or saucepan along with olive oil. Stir over medium heat for 5 minutes. Add tomato juice and herbs. Cover and simmer over medium heat for 20 minutes. Add zucchini, fish filets and shrimp or prawns. Cook for another 5 to 7 minutes.

Shell peas and steam until just done, about 3 to 4 minutes. Combine with cooked rice.

Serve paella on a bed of peas and rice.

Serves 4 to 6.

FISH

Marinated Asparagus with Crab

A special dish.

> 2 bunches fresh asparagus (the shortest fattest spears you can find!)
> 6 scallions, finely chopped
> 2 sprigs parsley, finely chopped
> 1 sprig fresh tarragon, finely chopped
> 2 Tbs. olive oil
> 3 Tbs. lemon juice
> 2 Tbs. apple cider vinegar
> 1/2 tsp. dry mustard
> 1/4 lb. loose crab meat
> 1 whole fresh crab, cleaned and cracked

Steam asparagus 7 to 10 minutes or until soft. Set aside in a large bowl and add scallions, parsley and tarragon.

Mix olive oil, lemon juice, vinegar and mustard and add to asparagus. Gently turn the asparagus in the marinade and refrigerate for at least one hour.

To serve, arrange asparagus on a flat platter, piled about 3 spears high and sprinkle loose crab meat on top. Cover with remaining marinade and arrange pieces of crab in shell around the outer edge of the platter. Add extra parsley sprigs for decoration.

Serves 4 to 6.

Grilled Butterfly Prawns

An extravagant dish!

> 2 lbs. large prawns, shelled
> 1/2 lb. large mushrooms, sliced 1/4"
>   thick
> 1/2 tsp. dry mustard
> 1/2 tsp. powdered rosemary
> 1/4 cup apple juice
> 1/2 tsp. toasted sesame oil
> 1 Tbs. rice wine vinegar

Butterfly prawns by splitting almost in two down the back. Press somewhat flat. Mix with mushrooms.

Using a small bowl, make a paste with the mustard, rosemary and a tablespoon or two of the apple juice. Add sesame oil and rice vinegar and mix well. Add remaining apple juice and mix again. Pour over prawns and mushrooms and marinate for 2 hours minimum, turning prawns and mushrooms frequently.

Alternate prawns and mushrooms on skewers. Grill over hot barbecue or hibachi coals for about five minutes, rotating the skewers slowly for even cooking.

Serves 4.

FISH

Mu Shu Shrimp

This Chinese dish is traditionally prepared along with scrambled eggs. I prefer to separate the shrimp from the eggs, occasionally serving the egg version for a special breakfast.

> 4 dried black mushrooms
> 1/2 cup hot water
> 2 tsp. toasted sesame oil (see *Cooking Notes*)
> 1 head Napa (Chinese) cabbage, shredded
> 2-7 oz. cans bamboo shoots, slivered
> 2 cloves garlic, minced
> 1/2 tsp. fresh ginger, grated
> 1/2 tsp. Chinese Five-Spice Powder (Five-Spice Powder is a combination of powdered fennel, ginger root, licorice root, cinnamon and cloves.)
> 1/2 lb. bay shrimp
> 4-5 green onions
> 1 package lumpia (spring roll) skins or 1 package flour tortillas

Soak mushrooms in hot water for a minimum of 5 minutes. Chop mushrooms into small pieces and reserve water.

Coat the bowl of a wok or large frying pan with the oil and set over high heat until oil just begins to smoke. Add shredded cabbage, chopped mushrooms, slivered bamboo shoots, garlic and ginger. Stir and toss quickly for 3 minutes.

Add mushroom–soaking water and Five–Spice Powder. Cover and steam for 5 minutes. Add shrimp and mix well. Steam for another 2 minutes and remove from heat.

Cut green onions in half width-wise, then slice into thin shreds. Place a few onion shreds in the center of each lumpia skin or tortilla, then place 2 heaping tablespoons of the shrimp mixture on top of the onions. Roll the skin or tortilla up tightly, folding in the sides.

Note: Lumpia skins need not be heated, but flour tortillas require *slight* warming before use.

Serves 6 to 8.

POULTRY

Chicken Tacos

1 frying chicken, boiled and skinned
2-3 leeks or scallions, finely chopped
1 avocado, peeled and chopped into
    small pieces
1/2 lb. mushrooms, sliced and steamed
Alfalfa sprouts
Corn tortillas, heated in a 400° oven

Taco sauce:
1/2 cup broth (see *Basic Chicken Broth*)
3 tomatoes
1/2 tsp. ground cumin
Cayenne pepper to taste

Combine sauce ingredients in a blender. Pour into a small saucepan and simmer for about 10 minutes. Remove from heat and allow to cool slightly as you assemble the tortillas.

Remove meat from cooked chicken and stuff into warmed tortillas with vegetables. Top with sauce.

Serves 4 to 6.

Chicken Tacos

Chicken Salad

This recipe can be served as a salad or as a delightful sandwich spread.

4 chicken breasts
1 Tbs. chopped chives
2 stalks celery, deveined
1/4 of small jicama
1/4 cup chicken broth (see *Basic Chicken Broth*)
2 lemon cucumbers, peeled and sliced
1 small-sized head romaine lettuce, shredded
4-5 leaves fresh sweet basil, minced
Chicken Broth Dressing (see *Salad Dressings*)

Steam chicken breasts 15 to 20 minutes or until tender. Discard skin and bones and break meat into chunks. Mince in a food processor along with chives, celery and jicama. (If you don't own a food processor, you may use a large, sharp knife for chopping.) Blend in chicken broth.

Mix cucumbers, lettuce and basil in a serving bowl. Add chicken mixture and salad dressing, and toss vigorously.

Serves 4.

Orange Chicken

A quick and easy meal to prepare for last minute guests.

> 4 chicken breasts skinned
> 6 chicken thighs, skinned
> 1/2 tsp. powdered oregano
> 2 pinches powdered cloves
> 1 orange
> 1-plus cup orange juice

Place chicken parts in the bottom of a baking dish. Sprinkle with oregano and cloves. Slice orange, with peel, into very thin rounds, and lay over chicken pieces.

Pour 1 cup orange juice into the bottom of the pan and bake, uncovered, in a preheated 350° oven for 25 to 30 minutes, checking liquid in bottom of pan occasionally. If the chicken seems dry, splash on another 1/2 cup of orange juice. Liquid should cook down considerably at the end of the cooking time, but glaze of liquid should remain to keep the chicken moist.

Serves 4 to 6.

POULTRY

Pineapple-Glazed Chicken

This dish is cooked on skewers over barbecue or hibachi coals, and can be served hot or cold. Skewers may be placed in the broiler for those who don't have access to a barbecue.

10-12 small white boiling onions, peeled and halved
8 chicken breasts, skinned and boned
4 green peppers, cut into 1" chunks
1-1 lb. can unsweetened pineapple chunks

Glaze:
3 cups unsweetened pineapple juice
2 Tbs. cornstarch
2 tsp. dry mustard

Prepare the glaze first, as it needs cooling time: warm pineapple juice in a saucepan over medium heat. Mix cornstarch and dry mustard together in a cup. Pour about 1/4 cup of the warm pineapple juice into the cup and mix until smooth, then return cornstarch mixture to the pineapple juice in the saucepan. Continue to cook over medium heat until mixture has thickened, about 15 minutes. Remove from heat and cool until thick enough to be applied to chicken with a basting brush.

Steam onions for about 5 minutes as you cut chicken into 1" by 2" chunks. Alternate chicken, pepper, onion and pineapple chunks on bamboo skewers.

Coat each loaded skewer with glaze and set on grill over very hot coals. (Do not crowd skewers too tightly.) Cook for 25 to 30 minutes, turning frequently and basting continuously with the glaze.

Serves 4.

POULTRY

Red Onion Chicken

Onion seeps into the chicken and gives this dish a wonderful flavor.

    8 chicken breasts, skinned and boned
      (save the skins)
    1 large red onion, chopped into 1/4" by
      1/2" pieces
    2 tsp. unsalted (sweet) butter

Lay chicken breasts out flat in a large baking pan. Cut about 6 to 8 small slits into the top of each breast and insert a piece of onion into each slit. Add a dot of butter (1/4 tsp.) to the top of each breast and cover with piece of chicken skin spread loosely over the butter and onion.

Bake in a preheated 350° oven for 15 minutes. Remove skins, then broil for 3 minutes to brown.

Serves 4 to 6.

Anise Chicken

This dish uses the anise bulb both as vegetable and flavoring. The sweet anise bulb also known as Florence fennel is seasonal and is available September through May. The bulb tastes very delicate, unlike the seeds.

> 1/2 tsp. oil or unsalted (sweet) butter
> 1 small yellow onion, peeled and sliced
> 12 chicken thighs, skinned
> 1/2 cup white or whole wheat flour
> 1 anise bulb
> 1 - 1 1/2 cups apple juice

Melt oil or butter in a large frying pan. Add peeled and finely sliced onion and brown slightly over medium-low heat. Coat chicken lightly with flour and brown with onions.

Prepare anise by slicing all stalks cleanly away from the bulb. Also slice off about 1/4" from the root end. Thinly slice the remaining bulb, and nestle into pan around the chicken pieces.

Turn chicken, onion and anise together in the pan, add 1 cup of apple juice and cover. Once the juice is simmering rapidly, reduce heat to very low. Cook for 1/2 hour, turning chicken once or twice. When pan juices are at a low point and are caramel brown in color, the chicken is ready to serve.

Serve plain or on a bed of brown rice.

Serves 6.

POULTRY

Chicken Curry

1 frying chicken, skinned and cut up
1 yellow onion, thinly sliced
1/2 lb. fresh mushrooms, sliced
1 Pippin apple, cored and sliced
1/2 cup apple juice or white wine
1 tsp. tarragon
2 tsp. curry powder (or more, according
   to taste)
1 Tbs. sesame seeds (optional)

Place all ingredients in a large saucepan. Cook covered, over low heat, for 45 minutes to an hour, adding extra liquid (apple juice or wine) as necessary. When chicken is done, transfer to a serving dish with half of the mushrooms, onions, and apple slices. Puree the other half of this vegetable-fruit mixture with the remaining liquid, in a blender. Pour over chicken pieces.

Serves 4.

Tomato Herb Chicken

This dish and a salad make a perfect light meal.

> 1 tsp. safflower oil
> 1 yellow onion, thinly sliced
> 5 medium-sized tomatoes, chopped
> 4 chicken breasts, skinned
> 1 cup unsalted tomato juice
> 1 1/2 tsp. bouquet garni or 1 tsp. sage
>   and 1/2 tsp. rosemary

Brown onion quickly in oiled frying pan. Add tomatoes and cook for 3 minutes.

Add chicken to pan, meaty side up. Pour tomato juice over chicken and sprinkle with herbs.

Cover and simmer for 1/2 hour, turning chicken once. If pan juices are low, add another 1/2 cup tomato juice 10 minutes before chicken is done.

Serves 4.

POULTRY

Chicken Stew with Corn Dumplings

The chicken and broth must be prepared the night before you plan to serve the stew.

> 1 whole chicken, cut up
> Water, enough to completely cover
>   chicken pieces
>
> 1 tsp. sweet basil
> 1/4 tsp. marjoram
> Pinch cayenne pepper
> 1 yellow onion, sliced
> 3 stalks celery, chopped
> 1 carrot, grated
> 1 green pepper, sliced
> 3 zucchini, sliced
> 2 cups small, fresh mushrooms, whole
>
> Dumplings:
> 1 cup fresh corn, cut from the cob
> 1 cup flour, sifted
> 1 1/2 tsp. low-sodium baking powder
>   (or 1 tsp. regular baking powder)
> 3 Tbs. corn meal
> 2 Tbs. minced parsley

The night before:
   Place chicken in very large saucepan or stockpot.

Cover with water and simmer, covered, for 2 hours. Remove from heat and transfer chicken pieces to a plate to cool. Remove meat and set aside in a bowl in the refrigerator. Cover the broth still in the cooking pot and refrigerate overnight.

To complete stew:

Skim the solidified chicken fat from the top of the broth and discard. Add herbs, cayenne pepper and sliced onion to the broth and simmer for 15 minutes over medium heat. Add prepared vegetables along with chicken meat. Continue to simmer stew while preparing dumplings.

Dumplings:

Blend fresh corn kernels in blender and place in bowl. Add corn meal. Sift flour and baking powder together and add to corn mixture. Add parsley and mix well. Dough should be very stiff, but if it seems dry, add water, 1/2 tsp. at a time.

Drop dough into the simmering stew, a heaping tablespoon at a time. Cover again and simmer for another 10 minutes. Serve immediately.

Serves 4 to 6.

POULTRY

Chicken and Sweet Rice Cabbage Rolls

Sweet or "glutinous" rice, when cooked, yields a sweeter, stickier result than white or brown rice, making it perfect for stuffing. This dish can be prepared ahead of time and reheated.

> 2 cups cooked sweet rice
> 1 head cabbage
> 4 chicken breasts, skinned, boned and ground in a food processor (or finely chopped)
> 1 small yellow onion, finely chopped
> 1 celery stalk, deveined and ground in a food processor (or finely chopped)
> 1/2 tsp. tarragon
> 1-2 cups broth (see *Basic Chicken Broth*)

To cook sweet rice, add 1 cup uncooked rice to 3 cups boiling water. Reduce heat and cook for 45 minutes or until water is absorbed and rice is soft and very sticky.

After removing the core, steam the cabbage for about 5 minutes until the leaves are soft but not so limp that they tear. Peel off 10 to 15 whole leaves.

Mix ground chicken, sweet rice, onion, celery and tarragon together in a large mixing bowl. Place 1 very heaping tablespoon of the chicken mixture onto the stem end of each cabbage leaf and roll, folding in the sides as you go.

Place cabbage rolls close together in a baking dish, with loose ends down. Add 1/2 to 1 cup chicken broth. Bake, uncovered, in a 350° oven for 30 to 40 minutes, basting occasionally. If liquid appears low, add more broth during baking time.

Serves 6.

POULTRY

Chicken Kiev

A more elaborate main dish, but well worth the effort.

> 4 chicken breasts, skinned, boned
>   and pounded flat
> 1 leek, very finely chopped
> 4 pinches sage
> 2 tsp. unsalted (sweet) butter (1/2 tsp.
>   per breast)
> 1 egg, beaten
> 1 cup flour
> 1 1/2 cups bread or cracker crumbs
>   (Make your own by putting toasted
>   bread or crackers through the
>   blender.)

Lay chicken pieces out flat and sprinkle with chopped leek and sage (1 pinch per breast), then place 1/2 tsp. of butter onto one end of each piece. Roll the chicken into tight rolls starting at the end with the butter.

Secure the outside end of each piece of chicken with one or two bamboo skewers. Dip each roll in beaten egg, then roll in flour, then in bread crumbs until completely coated.

Chill for 10 minutes, and preheat oven to 400°. Remove rolls from refrigerator, place in a large baking dish at least 2" apart, and bake uncovered for 25 to 30 minutes. Do not overcook.

Serves 4.

Chicken Kiev II

A very simple version with no added fat.

> 4 chicken breasts, skinned, boned and
>   pounded flat
> 1/4 cup fresh chives, chopped

Lay chicken flat and sprinkle with chopped chives. Roll, starting with the smaller end, making sure to wrap all of the chives tightly inside the roll. Secure with 2 wooden skewers, spearing through the outside end flap.

Steam in a large steamer for 20 to 25 minutes or until just done.

Serves 4.

POULTRY

Chicken Livers Español

This dish is very rich. Delicious served with rice or boiled white potatoes.

    1 tsp. safflower or peanut oil
    1 yellow onion, sliced
    1 lb. fresh chicken livers
    4 tomatoes, chopped into chunks
    1 cup unsalted tomato juice
    1 tsp. sweet basil
    2 cups fresh shelled peas or 1-10 oz.
      package frozen peas, thawed

Coat the bottom of a frying pan with oil. Brown onions lightly. Add livers and brown for 2 minutes, then add tomatoes, juice and sweet basil. Simmer over low heat for 8 minutes, turning frequently. Add peas and continue to cook, covered, for another 3 minutes.

Serves 4.

Sage Game Hens with Barley

As game hens are small, figure on one per person.

> 4 Rock Cornish game hens
> 1-1/2 tsp. sage
> 2–3 cups water
> 3 cups water or broth (see *Basic Chicken Broth*)
> 1 1/2 cups pearl barley

Split game hens in half. Lay in a baking pan, skin side up. (Do not crowd the halves or they will cook unevenly.) Sprinkle with sage.

Add 2 cups water to the baking pan. Bake in a preheated 350° oven for 30 to 40 minutes. While baking, splash once or twice with water to keep the meat moist and to prevent sticking.

While hens are baking, bring 3 cups water or broth to a boil in a saucepan. Add barley, return to a boil, then reduce heat to low and cook uncovered for 35 to 40 minutes or until barley is soft and all the liquid has been absorbed.

Serve hens on a bed of cooked barley.

Serves 4.

POULTRY

Stuffed Game Hens

Use one bird per person. This recipe allows for leftover stuffing.

> 1/2 cup wild rice
> 1/2 cup brown rice
> 2 stalks celery, finely chopped
> 2 shallots, minced
> 3 cups broth (see *Basic Chicken Broth*)
> 1 cup currants
> 2 tsp. grated lemon rind
> 1 1/2 tsp. thyme
> 6 Rock Cornish game hens

Cook wild and brown rice, celery and shallots in broth for approximately 45 minutes, or until all the broth has boiled away and the rice is tender. Add currants, lemon rind and thyme and mix well. If stuffing seems dry, add more chicken broth.

Stuff game hens and place on wire racks set into baking pans. Bake in a preheated 350° oven for 40 to 45 minutes, basting twice with chicken broth.

Serves 6.

Roast Capon with Buckwheat Stuffing

We use this recipe for holiday meals.

> 1 capon
> 2 cups cooked buckwheat groats
> 1-2 cups bread crumbs (You may use
> your own crumbled toast.)
> 1/3 cup chopped water chestnuts
> 1 small apple, cored and chopped into
> chunks
> 1/2 cup raisins
> 1 red onion
> 2 stalks celery
> 1/2 tsp. allspice
> 1 tsp. rosemary
> 1-2 cups broth (see *Basic Chicken Broth*)

Preheat oven to 400°.

Mix all ingredients (except capon) together in a large bowl. Stuff capon with this mixture.

Set capon onto a wire rack inside a large baking pan, add enough water to cover bottom of pan, and place into oven. *Immediately* reduce heat to 350°. Bake, allowing about 20 minutes per pound—usually around 2 hours will suffice for a normal-sized bird.

Serves 6 to 8.

DESSERTS

DESSERTS

Apple Gel

2 cups apple juice
1 cup water
1 stick kanten (see *Cooking Notes*)
1 large sweet apple (Golden Delicious, preferably), peeled, cored and thinly sliced

Pour juice and water into saucepan. Add kanten stick (you can snap it into pieces to fit into your pan) and bring to boil. Turn heat down to a low–simmer and continue to cook, stirring occasionally, until kanten has completely dissolved. (Mixture should cook for at least 20 minutes.)

Pour hot liquid mixture into a bowl, refrigerate for 5 to 10 minutes. Remove and decorate with apple slices. Return to refrigerator and chill for approximately 1/2 hour, or until completely set.

Serves 4.

Apple–Apricot Gel

Follow same instructions as above, substituting 1 cup unsweetened apricot nectar for one cup of the apple juice. Add a drop of vanilla extract and use 12 apricot halves for decoration.

Berry Delight

2 cups apple/boysenberry juice or
    apple juice
1 cup water
1 stick kanten (see *Cooking Notes*)
2 baskets fresh boysenberries or 1-lb.
    bag frozen boysenberries

Pour juice and water into saucepan. Add kanten stick, and soak for 5 minutes.

Add berries to saucepan and set over medium-low heat. When mixture comes to a boil, reduce heat even further and continue to cook for another 15 minutes, making sure kanten has dissolved completely. Pour into a serving bowl and refrigerate for 40 minutes or until completely set.

Serves 4.

DESSERTS

Pear-Almond Dessert Mold

3 cups pear juice
1 stick kanten (see *Cooking Notes*)
3 large pears, peeled, cored, steamed and pureed or
    1-lb. can unsweetened pears, pureed
1/4 tsp. almond extract
1/2 cup slivered almonds (optional)

Pour juice into saucepan and add kanten stick. Bring to a boil, turn heat down to low-simmer and continue to cook, stirring occasionally, until kanten has dissolved completely. (Mixture should cook for at least 20 minutes.)

Add pureed pears, cook for another 3 minutes and remove from heat. Stir in almond extract.

Pour into a serving bowl and chill in refrigerator for 5 to 10 minutes. Remove and top with slivered almonds. Return to refrigerator and chill for another 1/2 hour or until completely set.

Serves 4.

Date Tapioca Pudding

For this dessert, use the softest, largest dates you can find. I prefer the flavor of Medjool dates.

    3 cups low-fat or non-fat milk
    5-8 pitted dates
    2 egg yolks
    1/4 cup granulated tapioca
    1 tsp. vanilla
    1 egg white

Blend 1 cup of the milk with pitted dates in a blender. Pour mixture into a saucepan and add remaining 2 cups milk. Beat in egg yolks, mixing well.

Sprinkle tapioca over the date–milk–egg mixture. Let stand for 10 minutes, allowing the tapioca to soak. Cook over medium heat, stirring constantly, for 7-10 minutes or until mixture comes to a full boil. Remove from heat, stir in vanilla, and let cool for 5 minutes.

Beat egg white in a bowl until it forms stiff peaks. Fold quickly into tapioca. Chill in refrigerator for at least 4 hours.

Serves 4.

DESSERTS

Parfaits

Fruit can be combined with other dessert recipes to create fancy parfaits.

> 1 basket strawberries, sliced, or other
>   fresh or stewed fruit
> 1 recipe *Date Tapioca Pudding*

Prepare *Date Tapioca Pudding* as directed. Allow to cool only enough so that a piece of berry dropped into the tapioca does not sink, usually when the pudding is still warm, but *not* hot. Place 1" of chopped strawberries in the bottom of a glass. Add a 1" layer of tapioca, then another layer of strawberries. Continue layering until glass is full. Refrigerate at least 2 hours before serving.

Serves 8.

OR:

> 1 recipe *Berry Delight*
> 1 recipe *Date Tapioca Pudding*

Prepare recipes as directed. Allow each to cool until semi-solid, then alternate layers in a glass. Refrigerate for at least 2 hours before serving.

Serves 8.

Pear-Applesauce

This recipe makes a wonderful topping for hot cereal, toast or yogurt, and also is a good, light dessert.

> 10 good-sized apples (preferably Gravensteins), peeled, cored and cut into chunks
> 10 pears, peeled, cored and cut into chunks (ripe Bartletts work best)
> 2 tsp. cinnamon
> Juice from 1 lemon, optional
> 2 cups of apple juice
> 1/4 tsp. vanilla

Place all ingredients except lemon juice in a large saucepan. Use the lemon juice only to add zest to bland apples. Mix in spice, then cook over medium heat until liquid comes to a boil. Turn heat to low and simmer, covered, for 20 to 30 minutes, or until fruit has softened. Mash with potato masher or fork. Drain off excess liquid and chill.

Serves 6.

DESSERTS

Stewed Fruit

An easy-to-prepare, low-calorie dessert. Be sure to choose ripe fruit.

> Fresh fruit
> 1/2 cup fruit juice (approximately)

Simmer fruit for 2 to 5 minutes in just enough juice to moisten. Chill.

Note: Plums, peaches, apricots, figs, cherries and berries are best for stewing. Because of their firmer texture, apples and pears cook better when steamed rather than stewed.

Fresh Fruit Frappé

A refreshing dessert drink or topping for your breakfast cereal.

 6 ozs. low-fat or non-fat milk
 1 egg
Plus one of the following:
 1/2 papaya
 1 banana
 1/2 basket (1 cup) fresh blueberries
 1 cup stewed apricots
 1 tsp. vanilla (optional)

Puree ingredients in a blender and serve.

Serves 1 to 2.

DESSERTS

Steamed Pears with Boysenberry Sauce

Blackberries may be substituted if boysenberries are unavailable.

> 4 large fresh pears, peeled and cored
> 2 cups apple/berry or apple juice
> 2 Tbs. cornstarch
> 1-lb. package frozen boysenberries or
>   1 lb. fresh boysenberries

Stew or steam pears for 2 to 5 minutes (depending on size) until easily pierced with a fork, but still firm. Cut pears in half, place on a plate and chill in refrigerator.

Pour juice into a saucepan and cook over medium heat until just warm. Spoon about 1/4 cup of the juice from the saucepan into a cup and mix in cornstarch. Stir until smooth.

Add berries to juice in saucepan, then add cornstarch mixture. Continue to cook over medium heat, stirring constantly, until sauce has thickened to a syrupy consistency.

Serve warm berry sauce over pears.

Serves 4.

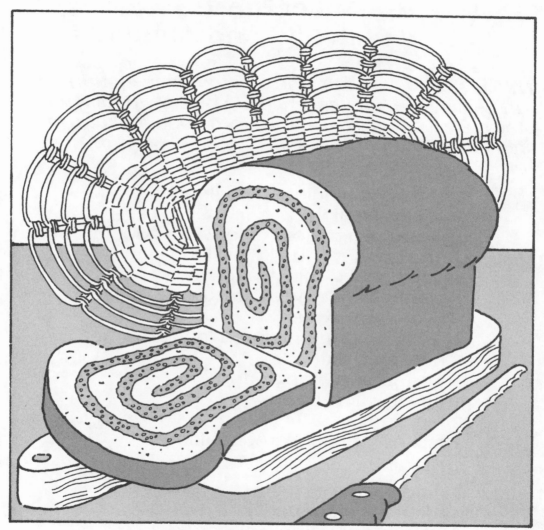

Millet Bread Filled with Figs and Almonds

DESSERTS

Millet Bread
Filled with Figs and Almonds

This recipe takes time, and it is worth every minute. It can be served as a dessert, plain or topped with whipping cream or low-fat milk tapioca. Also makes a great breakfast roll when toasted!

Bread:
1 1/2 cups whole wheat flour
1 cup millet flour
1/4 cup gluten flour (use white flour if you cannot find gluten flour)
1 cup cooked millet, packed
1 Tbs. active dry yeast, mixed in 1/4 cup lukewarm water
1/2 cup yogurt or soured low-fat or non-fat milk
1 Tbs. grated orange rind
1 egg, beaten
2 tsp. vanilla
1 tsp. oil (apricot kernel, safflower, peanut)

Filling:
12 fresh figs, stewed
3 oz. almonds, finely chopped

To prepare filling, stew figs for about 5 minutes. Drain off liquid and mash. Chop almonds and mix into figs. Set aside.

Mix the flours and cooked millet together in a large mixing bowl. Add yogurt, egg, vanilla and oil to the yeast-water mixture, then add to the dry ingredients. Mix well.

Turn dough out onto a lightly floured board and knead for about 5 minutes. Place into a buttered bowl, cover with a dry clean dish towel and let rise in a warm (70°) place for 1 1/4 hours, or until doubled in bulk.

Turn dough once again onto floured board, punch down, then pat and stretch into a rectangle about 9" wide, 20" long and 3/4" thick.

Spoon the fig mixture onto the dough, distributing it evenly up to the edges of the rectangle. Starting at one 9" end, gently roll up the dough, and pinch ends to secure filling inside. Place in an oiled loaf pan and let rise again for another hour or so.

Bake in a preheated 350° oven for 45 minutes. Allow bread to cool for 20 minutes before removing from pan.

Serves 8 to 10.

DESSERTS

Fig-Stuffed Baked Apples

A hearty cold weather dessert.

> 6 Pippin apples
> 12 fresh figs, chopped
> 2 oz. unsalted pecans, chopped
> 1/2 tsp. cinnamon
> 1/2 cup apple juice
> 1/2 pt. whipping cream or 1/2 pt. yogurt
>   or 1/4 lb. grated, unsalted goat's
>   cheese (optional)

Preheat oven to 375°. Core apples, allowing extra space for the stuffing. Mix together chopped figs and pecans and sprinkle with cinnamon. Stuff the apples, packing the fig mixture in tightly.

Stand apples upright in the juice and bake in a covered baking dish for about 30 minutes. Serve hot, topped with cream, yogurt or goat's cheese, if desired.

Serves 6.

Fig-Stuffed Baked Apples

DESSERTS

Fantastic Fresh Fig Torte

Very, very rich! For special occasions only.

Spongecake:
5 Tbs. unsalted (sweet) butter
6 eggs, separated
3 tsp. vanilla
3/4 cup millet flour or white flour
3/4 cup whole wheat flour

Filling:
2 baskets ripe purple figs, stewed
1/3 cup unsalted pecans, finely
    chopped
1/2 pt. heavy cream, whipped

To prepare filling, stew figs and drain off excess liquid. Mash thoroughly. Mix in chopped pecans and set aside to cool.

Melt butter and set aside. Whip egg yolks with the vanilla until they appear thick and creamy. Whip egg whites in a separate bowl until stiff.

Sift flours together and slowly fold into egg yolk mixture, alternating with scoops of the egg whites. Do not over-mix. Fold in the cooled, melted butter.

Pour into a round, 10" false-bottomed cake pan, distributing mixture evenly. Bake in a preheated 350° oven for 20 to 25 minutes. Cool for 10 minutes and remove from pan. Allow to cool completely before assembling torte.

To assemble the torte, slice cake in half width-wise, making two thin layers. (As the cake itself will not have risen more than a few inches, each layer will be only 1/2" to 3/4" thick.) Place bottom layer on a flat serving platter. Cover with thoroughly cooled fig mixture. Add 1/2 of the whipped cream, spreading it evenly over the figs. Place second layer of cake on top of the cream, then frost the top of the second layer lightly with remaining cream. Decorate the top layer with a few pecan halves or stewed, halved figs. Allow to chill in refrigerator for at least one hour before serving.

Serves 8.

DESSERTS

Fresh Mango Pie

This dessert has a wonderful, delicate flavor and not a bit of fat!

Filling:
3 large, ripe mangoes, peeled
1 cup non-fat milk
3 Tbs. cornstarch

Crust:
5 unsalted rice cakes or 2 1/2 · 3 cups
    unsalted puffed rice
4 egg whites
1/4 tsp. nutmeg

Break rice cakes into chunks and crush in blender to a fine powder. Whip egg whites with an egg beater or wire whip until they form stiff peaks. Pour rice cake "powder" onto egg white and sprinkle with nutmeg. Mix well to form a spongy dough.

Spoon into an 8" pie plate, patting the dough flat with a spatula or spoon back. (Though dough wil appear grainy and rough, after it is baked, it has a meringue-like texture.)

Bake in a preheated, 350° oven for 12 minutes. Remove from oven and let cool while preparing filling.

Slice meat away from pit of two mangoes, and drop into blender. Add milk and puree. Add milk as necessary so that mango and milk combined measure 2 cups.

Pour 1/4 cup of the mango and milk mixture into a cup and add cornstarch. Stir until smooth and put in saucepan. Heat remaining mango and milk mixture slightly and slowly add to cornstarch mixture, stirring well. Cook over very low heat for 15 minutes, stirring constantly. (Heating the mango–milk mixture before adding to the cornstarch mixture helps it to blend and thicken smoothly.)

Slice the remaining mango into thin slices and place on baked crust. Pour the cooked mixture over the mango. Let cool slightly, then chill in refrigerator for at least 3 hours, or until cooked mixture has set.

Serves 4 to 6.

DESSERTS

Apricot-Stuffed Rolls

Ideal for a special Sunday brunch or breakfast in bed.

Dough:
1 very soft date, pitted
1/2 cup boiling water
1 Tbs. active dry yeast
3/4 cup low-fat or non-fat milk
2 Tbs. unsalted (sweet) butter
1 1/2 cups whole wheat flour
1 1/2 cups white flour
15 large, ripe apricots or 1-29 oz. can whole, unsweetened apricots
1 cup low-fat or non-fat cottage cheese (1/2 cup golden raisins, if preferred)
1 tsp. cinnamon

Begin by preparing dough. Soak pitted date in boiled water for 15 minutes. Puree date and water in a blender. Measure 1/4 cup of the date-water into a bowl, then add yeast and dissolve thoroughly. Heat milk and butter in saucepan until butter melts. Cool to lukewarm and gently add the yeast-date mixture. Stir in the flour. Roll dough into a ball, place in a bowl, cover and let rise until doubled in bulk, about one hour.

Wash and pit apricots, keeping whole. (If the apricots are very ripe, the pits can be removed easily without splitting the fruit.)

Mix the cinnamon with the cottage cheese. Stuff the center of each apricot with cottage cheese–cinnamon mixture or with the golden raisins if you choose to omit the cottage cheese. Set aside.

Break off 15 chunks of dough of equal size and roll into balls, then into flat circles, about 1/4" thick. Place one apricot in the center of each dough circle and gather the circle up around the apricot, pinching the dough together to close the seam.

Place rolls on a large, greased baking sheet, cover with a clean dish towel and let rise again until doubled in bulk, about one hour.

Bake in a preheated 400° oven until golden brown, about 15 minutes.

Serves 6.

DESSERTS

Glazed Apple Cake

Glazed Apple Cake

A great coffee cake.

> 1 3/4 cups whole wheat or rye flour
> 3/4 cup rice flour
> 1 Tbs. low-sodium baking powder
> 1/2 tsp. cardamon
> 1/2 tsp. nutmeg
> 1 cup unsweetened applesauce
> 5 large dates (pitted Medjool dates work
>   best)
> 1/2 cup hot water
> 2 Tbs. melted unsalted (sweet) butter or
>   safflower oil
> 2 apples, peeled, cored and thinly
>   sliced
> 2 cups apple juice

Mix flours, baking powder and spices together in a large bowl. Blend applesauce, dates, water and melted butter or oil in a blender. Slowly mix wet ingredients into dry.

Grease and flour high-rimmed round cake or bundt pan. Overlap apple slices from one apple in a ring on the bottom of the pan. Spoon 1/2 of the dough over the apples. Lay remaining apple slices in a ring over first layer of dough. Spoon on remaining dough.

(continued on next page)

DESSERTS

Bake in a preheated 350°oven for 40 minutes.

Boil 2 cups apple juice until reduced by 1/2. Juice should thicken into a syrup when removed from heat for a minute or two.

Remove cake from pan while still hot. Pour apple syrup over the cake. Serve warm.

Serves 8.